WITHIN THE WOMB OF GOD

WITHIN THE WOMB OF GOD

FROM THE JOURNALS AND WRITINGS OF DIANNE WULTZEN KELTER, CERTIFIED PASTORAL MINISTER AND LIFE COACH

DIANNE KELTER

To order additional copies of this book, contact:
Xlibris
1-888-795-4274
www.Xlibris.com
Orders@Xlibris.com
794086

CONTENTS

For like a baby in a womb whose life is sustained by its mother,
I am in the womb of God, and it is there I am sustained.
Dianne, 1998

This book is dedicated to our Lord, Jesus Christ, and all the angels he sent to help and guide me on my journey.

Some of my angels include:

My family: you, besides Jesus the Christ, are my rock of stability and love.

My friends: your support and laughter gave me strength.

My spiritual guides and mentors, parish pastors, and priests: thank you for all the lessons and guidance I received from working with you. All of your lectures, retreats, or books brought me deeper into my relationship with Christ.

Thank you,
Dianne
August 2019

Preface

Even though my story is not unique, it is intensely personal, and it has always been difficult to share. However, it is through sharing just such a journey that I have been able to assist others in overcoming their own crises in life and faith. At the same time, I find that my own faith strengthens and enhances my intimate relationship with God, and I can testify He is alive because I have seen Him myself. That is why having faith in God is the most important aspect of our lives.

This book will show you how to find Christ in your life not only in adversity but in the good times. You will be able to see how to journal your life, because it started before you were born. I hope you will sit down and write your story. As you read my life, you will notice how my journal entries stem from my life. When you write your life, you will see where God was with you, where He talked to you, whom God sent to teach you to be strong, or and when He made you feel weak. You will see how your life is important. We are all on a journey. It is our journey of life that leads us back to before we were born.

My goals are to be a true disciple of Christ and a servant of God and His people.

> To serve, not be served.
> To see Christ in all.
> To answer God's call. To love all!

Is it easy? No! There are so many twists and turns. There's so much to learn, so much to experience. But I feel through our Lord Jesus Christ that I can do it.

When I have regrets and look back, I see where I would have missed so much of the life to which I was called. In my story, you will see that the choices that were painful gave me experiences of strength I didn't know I had. They gave me the understanding to be able to reach out to others with empathy and the listening skills to hear their story.

In Chapter 1, I tell my story. This is important because it tells the story of how I came to be. My Potter had already started to form me before I was born. Throughout my story, you will see how my future was already being formed. From how to fight for myself to the wisdom of my ancestors, to the importance of my faith and how my faith would teach me how to live.

At some point, I hope you will write your story and see where the Potter began to mold you!

Reflection

Easter Sunday, April 21, 2019

He has risen! Alleluia. The words spring forward in the prayers, songs, symbols, and greeting cards. He has risen. The Paschal mystery. Our Lord's death and resurrection. This is a time to celebrate. This is a time to believe. This is the moment of love, a love that is given repeatedly by God. Though the death of Jesus the Christ and His resurrection, we now have eternal life, if we so choose.

What does it take? An unconditional love. A love that goes deeper that we can imagine. A love that our mortal minds have a tough time wrapping our heads around. Why is this so hard? It's simple. Our ego gets in the way. The ego has been getting in the way since the beginning of time. How do we follow the Word made flesh, from His birth to His death to His resurrection to eternal life? How do we do this if we think we have to be in control, or we think we have all the answers, or we think we are better and smarter? How do we become one with each other? How do the many parts become one body if we don't see there are other parts? What if the other parts don't think or pray like we do? What if the other parts are poor or rich or not the same? How are we supposed to know what to do? Scripture tells us. What if that is wrong, or translated wrong? What if, what if—a million excuses to not let go of our ego.

What would you say if I told you that my ancestors and your ancestors have set blueprints for us? God's blueprints for each and every one of us. An individual blueprint designed just for us. We can start with Scripture, but you will see it then carries to our families and then our life experiences. I invite you to follow my journey as I show you how track your own journey. We will see our ups and downs, our traumas and triumphs. We will see how our lives give us choices and how God never leaves us alone. He loves us all individually but also as one. God loves us enough to never part from us, not even after our earthly death. Because our God loves in a way our mortal minds cannot comprehend. So take my hand and let us walk into this great oneness together. Alleluia.

Dianne

My Potter

My Potter carefully crafted me in His image.

Through His handiwork, He instilled in me what was needed to fulfill his purpose. I was given the ones who would guide me. I was given the words of the old. He gave me the Word made flesh to guide me. He gave me the Holy Spirit to flow in and out of me with wisdom and guidance. I was given a canvas of beauty to surround me. The hardest part? I was given free will so I could choose my destination. The most important of all, He gave me unconditional love, a love so deep it is beyond mortal comprehension. He gave me a love that even in sin, He forgave, and through His son, Jesus the Christ, He gave me eternal life. First, I have a journey to take, a journey that is my special piece of the tapestry of life out of the clay He made me. So begins my journey.

Dianne
February 2018

Chapter 1

The Beginning

On a chilly November morning in Illinois, I entered this world. November 5, 1955 was the beginning of my earthly journey. My parents, Jeanne and Lavern (Fuzz), welcomed me, their first child, with open arms. They quickly introduced me to the other members of my family, my grandparents, aunts, uncles, cousins, and friends. They would be the ones, along with my parents, who would begin the journey with me on my path of life. Over the years, many others joined this journey. Fourteen months after I was born, my brother was born, and seven years later came my sister. My parents baptized me, and I began my faith journey as a follower of Jesus Christ.

I come from a diverse and strong family line. My great-grandmother Kate was left a widow with three children. She raised her children not only with great strength but also with pride and dignity. Years later, she remarried and raised two more children. The qualities of strength, determination, and dignity were passed down to all of us. My Grandmother Marie (Kate's daughter) was a great role model to me. Her humor and guidance provided me with the example of how I wanted to view life. I wanted to be as great a grandmother as she was. My mother, Jeanne, was a combination of both strong women before her. Her determination, her love of adventure, her love of others, and her caring skills as a registered nurse were gifts that she passed to me. All three women gave me the gift of my faith. The prayers and words were important, but not as important as their actions. I spent many hours with my mother and grandmother visiting the elderly or knitting rosary cases for the nursing home residents. Some days we would visit the families who'd lost a loved one. My mother and grandmother were always taking food to their homes. Other days, I would sit and listen to their stories—my favorite! Little did I know that they were laying the blueprints of my life.

The best of times was spent with all my aunts, uncles, and cousins congregated at my grandparents' home. This was the core, the center of our family. As the families grew, their home would be bursting at the seams. My paternal grandparents were just as strong. My grandfather William died of cancer when my grandmother Lydia was seven months pregnant with my uncle. She also had three other young children at home, my two aunts and my father. Later, Grandmother Lydia married a quiet, good man, Ross, whom I knew as Grandpa. My grandmother was a strong woman who barely laughed but taught me about listening.

My grandfather loved to garden, and my grandmother canned, baked, and utilized all he grew. When I was young, I thought my grandfather had the biggest garden; it seemed to go for miles. It wasn't until I went back as an adult that I realized how small it actually was. There was everything in that garden. In the front were strawberries, blueberries, raspberries, and blackberries and they were the sweetest berries I have ever tasted. Behind the berries were vegetables—lettuce, carrots, potatoes, beans, cucumbers, squash, cabbage, and tomatoes. Along the back were rows of sweet corn and popcorn.

My grandfather used an old push tiller to plow the ground. When we went over there or spent the night, we would help in the garden, and there is nothing sweeter than picking a berry and popping it in your mouth. I was fascinated with the carrots because they were underground just like the potatoes. When we harvested them, I got to dig in the dirt to find the orange jewels. There is something special about fruits and vegetables right out of a garden, and theirs was extra special. The cucumbers made the best pickles, and the fruit made jams that melted in your mouth. The sweet corn was so sweet and sitting and husking the popcorn made a double treat: not only did I get to sit and listen to the stories of my grandparents, but later my dad would pop the popcorn! Many lessons were learned snapping beans and opening pea pods.

My father served in World War II. He would never talk about it until right before he died. He served in the Pacific and was at the bottom of the hill in Iwo Jima. The lessons I learned from my family are richer than gold.

As I entered ministry, I began to see how my life mirrored Scripture. The lessons learned from my family brought me to understand not only the message but how to live it. From life to death, I learned not only how to face a problem but how to get to its root. I learned how to take the fruits of life (our gifts) and not only share them but expand them. From looking evil in the face and standing up for God. But most significantly, I learned how important it is to nurture our relationships with each other and with God. For it was and is through God that we are sustained!

> *Dreams are accomplished by the wisdom of the old and the courage of the youth. One without the other is just a fantasy. Dare to dream with wisdom and follow through with courage.*

> —*Dianne, November 4, 1998*

Chapter 2

MY RELATIONSHIP WITH GOD

Who am I? I am you, I am your neighbor, I am the store clerk, I am the bus driver, I am the person walking down the street. I am a person on a journey! Every one of us in this world is on the journey of life. My story is no more special and no less than anyone else. We are unique individuals with a purpose.

My purpose right now is to tell you about my relationship with God. You see, without God, I wouldn't be here. Without God, I would not have a purpose. Without God, I would never have survived my adversities.

One of my first memories when I was around four or five. It was Christmastime, and a neighbor brought us a beautiful wreath made from hard candy. While my mother was talking to a friend of my grandmother's, I reached up, pulled a piece of candy off the wreath, and popped it in my mouth. Suddenly I could not breathe. I remember my mother grabbing me, turning me upside down, and hitting my back, but nothing hurt, and I kept thinking, *I am okay.* Everyone was upset. My mom's friend looked like she was going to cry. My father was running around getting towels, and my mother kept hitting my back and sticking her fingers down my throat. I stayed there watching all this going on. I kept saying, "I'm okay," and then suddenly I wasn't okay—I hurt. My throat hurt, I was upside down, and in the towel was the candy. Everyone was crying now, including me. After I was put down, I walked over to my toys and started playing, trying to figure it all out. As far as that moment changing me, I don't know, but I do know I always had a closeness to the blessed Mother, and church was fascinating to me. There was something that drew me to it at a very young age.

A few years later, I had an experience that did change me, an experience that to this day is still fresh in my mind and that defined who I was as a person until I released it twenty years later. I was five, and the teenage boy convinced me and a friend to come into the basement of his house. When we got down there, two other boys were there. One of them locked the door, and the other told us to pull down our pants. I refused, and the one the boys went over and opened the door to the coal furnace. All I could see was the bright fire. We were scared, so we did what they said. After they were done, they opened the door to the furnace again and told us if we told anyone, they would find us and throw us in the furnace, and no one would find us. I ran home and never told anyone, but I knew I'd sinned, and I kept praying and telling God I was sorry.

It wasn't until years later that I told my mom. I was in sixth grade by then, and I was about to be confirmed. My teacher that year was a ninety-year-old nun who told our class to make sure we went confession because if we had any sins, the sacrament wouldn't take. Well, I worked up the courage and told my mother. I figured I was safe from the boys because they'd moved away a long time back. After I told her, she told me I did not sin and not to worry about it, but I did worry about it for a long time. I had nightmares, was always smelling smoke, and was afraid of fire. My mother gave me a rosary and told me when I was afraid, I should hold it and pray. I still do, to this day.

The Complete

The mortal mind cannot comprehend the mystery of God. We must move our mortal beings to a realm much deeper that ourselves. As we journey to the realm, the boundaries of mortality will attempt to impede our journey. It is with faith that we break the boundaries, and with courage that we prevail. The journey is long and tiresome, but the destination is complete. We must surrender our mortality and be lifted beyond the realms of mortal illusions, for it is these illusions that cloud the boundaries so we cannot cross. Until we leave behind the mortal illusions, we cannot enter into the, complete which is God. We are all called into the complete!

—Dianne, June 2002

Chapter 3

My Introduction to Ministry

When I was in seventh grade, I joined the Junior Legion of Mary. Every week, we chose an assignment. My choice was visiting the shut-ins. It was here that I could sit and listen to their stories for hours. One lady was a little bitty thing, and she lived in a house built into rock. She would always be in her bedroom, and a soft light filled her room. On her walls were hundreds of holy cards that covered her wall like wallpaper. One day she asked me to fix her a peanut butter sandwich because she was too sick to get up. When I went to the kitchen, there was no food, just a little peanut butter and some bread. I made her the sandwich and asked her if I could go get her some food, but she said she would be fine. When I left, I went to my grandmother's, who lived at the end of the alley, and asked her to please make Mary some of her soup.

Life continued, but I was having a lot of trouble in school. No matter how hard I tried, I could not get math. Spelling was hard too because I was always switching letters around. Reading was my highpoint. I loved to read because I could be anyone I wanted, and I was taught a new way of reading where one could speed-read but look for the main parts. We lived near the library, and I loved it. I would get books about history or my favorite books about the saints.

I would rather read than go outside to play, but my mom believed in moderation. Many a night, the flashlight would come out, and I would read most of the night. Of course, then I didn't want to get up for school.

The years rolled on, and before I knew it, I was in eighth grade and preparing for high school. It was around this time I got my lesson on betrayal by a friend—or in this case, friends. A girl in class did not like me and made fun of me all the time. I soon came to realize I was the butt of many jokes. I was determined to not let this bother me until it became known that anyone who hung around with me would be made fun of too. My friends started to ignore me and did not want to hang out with me at school. I was devastated. Once more I held it in and did not mention it; it was my problem. It was a given that after I graduated from Catholic grade school, I would go to the Catholic high school. The only problem was all my so-called friends were going there. I made the decision that instead of going to the school across the street, I was going to walk in the cold and snow to the other side of town. I had to walk because with one car in our family, I didn't have a choice. I knew I could do it. Besides, I reasoned, it would save my parents money. Much to my family's surprise and dismay, I announced I was going to the public high school. I never did tell them why. My parents chalked it up to me being stubborn and rebellious. Even though I forgave my friends, I could never forget, so I found myself somewhat distant. I had a hard time getting close to anyone. I was uncomfortable dating, so I avoided it. I loved high school and made new friends, both boys and girls. Somehow, I turned into a friend whom others could talk to about their problems if they needed someone to listen to them. I liked this role because I felt wanted and needed.

Perception

It is not about how others perceive you. It is about how you perceive yourself.

Only God and you know who you are. Others are just guessing.

Look deep inside yourself and see the beauty of who you are, and live out that beauty, for that is your true self.

Everything else is a perception of the true you!

—Dianne, August 2005

Chapter 4

Loss

During this time in my life, tragedy struck our family. I was fifteen and was a candy stripe at our local hospital. On this day, my grandmother, who had been sick off and on, was back in the hospital. I walked into her room to see how she was doing, and she was upset. She kept telling me my uncle was dead. I kept reassuring her he was fine; he had been visiting her but had to head home. She kept saying he was here, and now he was dead. I went to call my mother, but I got a page to come to the front office. I told my grandmother I would be right back. I ran down the hall, and when I got there, I saw my mother. I was so glad and told her she had to go talk to Grandma because she was upset. She said no and pulled me outside. I started arguing with her that she needed to go back. Suddenly my mother started crying and said, "Your uncle was killed in a car accident on his way home." She didn't want Grandma to know because she didn't feel she could handle the news, and she couldn't lose her mother and brother the same day. I tried explaining that my grandmother knew, but my family's grief was too much to comprehend my words.

The next several months changed the dynamic of our family. The funeral was a time of shock and disbelief. It wasn't until years later that this period set the path for my future in ministry. I remember going to sit in a room where my aunt was, and I asked her if I could get her something. She said, "No, but you could sit with me." Then she continued. "I just can't talk anymore."

Later, when they told my grandmother that my uncle died, she told my mom, "I know."

All too soon, my senior year rolled around, I was hit with a situation that once more defined me. While hanging out with a group of our friends, a handsome older guy showed up with some more friends. He had a car and gave us a ride home. I felt special because he saved me until last. I could not believe someone like him would want to be with me. He asked whether I had to get home, or whether we could go talk. We went to the football field near my house and talked. Suddenly he started kissing me, and I could not believe it. Not only did he want to be with me, but here I was parking and kissing this guy! Things started getting a little out of hand, and I tried to stop it, but he overpowered me and raped me. Outside the car, he pushed me up to the car and said, "Don't bother telling anyone. No one will believe you. You are a nothing." He took off, and I ran home vomiting. I did not want anyone to know. I couldn't be rejected again. When I got home, I was lucky: I made it upstairs without seeing anyone. I went to the bathroom took a handful of my mom's valium; she'd been put on this after my uncle had died. I did not want to live, but something told me to spit them out, and I did. He was not worth dying for. And I never told anyone.

Once more the pattern of holding in things continued. Coping did not work, and soon my behavior changed. I started drinking, smoking, and taking risks. While trying to deal with this internal personal hell, my grandmother, who was my best friend, mentor, and role model, died. A little over a month before I graduated, my life fell apart.

Summer was spent trying to find a job and debating whether I wanted to go to the junior college that had just opened. I decided on a job and part-time school. One day I was planning on going on a picnic with friends when the phone rang. On the other end were paramedics, and they wanted to talk to my mother. I explained she and other family members were out of town; they would be gone all day to help my aunt with a move. They proceeded to tell me my grandfather had fallen and refused to go to the hospital. I told them I would be right over. Thoughts of my grandfather filled my head as I ran to his house.

My grandfather was well-known and well liked throughout the community. I used to joke that my grandfather would be at my house with the news I did something wrong before I did it! When one grows up in a relatively small town, everyone knows everything and everyone, so I could get away with nothing— but then, common sense on my part might have helped. I found out that the nuns would call him whenever I decided I wanted a cigarette. I would go to the grotto at the convent across the street to sneak it. I cannot help but laugh at that lack of judgment on my part. Anyway, I knew my grandfather was having a hard time after losing his son and then his wife.

One day right after my grandmother died, my grandfather came to our house and asked if I would fix him breakfast. This was the first clue he was having some difficulty because everyone knew I was not a cook. I began the task of trying to crack the eggs into a bowl and carefully picking out the shells. He sadly said, "Fifty-one years ago tomorrow, I walked your grandmother down the aisle, and I promised God I would always take care of her. Now tomorrow, I will walk her down the aisle, only this time I will ask God to take care of her." Then he cried. I hugged him as I served him breakfast, and through his tears he started laughing. He looked at me and said, "Dia [his nickname for me]. how did you burn the outside of the eggs, yet the inside is cold?" He laughed and left for a restaurant.

These memories pounded in my head as I ran faster to his house. When I got to the open door, I stopped in shock. There in a chair was my hero, my grandfather. In his hand was a bottle of whiskey, and around his feet were empty cans of beer. The smell of urine and vomit filled the room. I told the police and paramedics I would handle it, and I set about the task of cleaning up him and the mess. Once more, even in this great state of grief, he gave me advice I never forgot. He said, "Dia, never forget this: it takes years to build a good reputation and only a few minutes to destroy it." He started to cry. He lived this hell for another seven years. In September 1980, he died peacefully praying the "Our Father." He was my grandpa, but later I realized he showed me Christ. Christ, in the whole man, the teacher. Christ, in the broken man, the passion and death. In my grandfather's dying, he rose with Christ in the resurrection.

Faith n Adversity

Faith is putting your trust in God and accepting his choices. This is difficult at times because sometimes it hurts, and deep. But there is learning from hurts. You can take on others' pain because you have been there, and you can feel their pain. If you use them properly, hurts teach you love. Love is the giving of yourself to others. Hurts also determine your faith. When Jesus was in the desert, He hurt, and He felt pain. We tend to forget He was human. He was tempted, we know, this because He listened to the devil. However, Jesus did not follow him—He challenged him. Jesus won because of His faith in His Father. We must challenge the devil when we are tempted by our hurts and pain. It was not easy for Jesus, and it is not easy for us.

Earlier this week, I was filled self-pity. Everyone hurt me, and I felt alone and fearful. I let my fears and my hurts overwhelm me. This caused anguish all around me. I had to look inside of me to see where I was wrong. And what I needed was my faith. I turned it over to God, and He helped me to overcome. I apologized, but I learned I must be more patient. If I am going to follow Christ, I must do it with love and fight for my faith. Like Jesus did. We are our own worst enemies when it comes to our faith. We believe that if anyone challenges us our faith, we will proclaim our belief. But we challenge our beliefs every day when we try to control our lives. We are saying we don't believe because we can handle it ourselves. When we trust in God, even if it takes a long time, we have faith.

Please, dear Lord, give me the strength and wisdom to follow and trust in You always. Let me feel and show the intimacy of Your love and grace. Amen.

Dianne, November 1998

Chapter 5

CAREERS

My careers are another part of who I am. My first big career encompassed the lessons of life I had learned so far, but then my world expanded. I began as an apprentice in respiratory therapy and received my training through the hospital. Later, I went to a community college and received my certification as an EMT. One of the highlights of this program was that I scored the second highest in the state of Illinois on my boards. This was a shock because of my dyslexia and learning difficulties.

During my twelve years at the hospital, one of my roles was resuscitation. It was here that I learned several things. First, if it is your time to die, no matter how much equipment or how many professionals there are, it is your time. One night we had a young man come in who'd had a heart attack. We worked on him for a long time and brought him back. He was furious with us. He told us how peaceful he was and how much pain he was in then. He told us if he went again, we should not bring him back. That was the first time I knew of someone other than me having died and come back. Though my death was a short time, he described the peace I'd had when I'd choked on the candy. There are so many times that death was shown to me. Some lived on; others went on to God. Their lives were never forgotten. The hardest parts were the children. The other thing I learned is even if you think you know your path in life, that's not it.

From there I went on to be coordinator of pastoral ministry in various churches. I also had the opportunity to develop support groups for individuals who were blind.

These experiences provided me the opportunity to become the first female police chaplain for our city.

As you can see, God had set my path. I simply did not know what it was.

Lord, Help Me

Lord, help me to be the best I can be in thought, word, and action. Let my life portray Your image in all that I say and do. Help me to show others the love You have for them. Amen.

Dianne, January 12, 1998

In 1975, right before Christmas, my brother arrived at my apartment. He was home from college and wanted to hang out. I drove because he didn't have a car, and we went to the old hangouts.

The first stop was a hit. All his friends were there, and because we were close in age, we knew each other's friends. It was fun catching up. Not only did we have fun with old friends, but he introduced me to a new friend. This friend ended up being my husband in 1977. Unfortunately, the marriage ended in 1997. The details are very difficult. I trusted, and once more I felt destroyed. We had five children together, but it was a difficult time. My father passed away in 1994. In 1996, my health started to fail, and after numerous tests, the only thing that showed was stress. Everyone thought it was due to my father's death, and it partly was, but I had other secrets from my past that I kept inside me for twenty years. My doctors had me take classes on biofeedback and meditation, and finally I went to counseling sessions. It was during this time that I learned I had three to five years to live because my body was shutting down due to the stress. I learned I had to recall the situations in my life and release them. When the divorce was final, I had to find different ways to deal with the stress of running a home and raising five children alone. Now, twenty years later at the time of this writing, I've survived.

My Inner Self

Sometimes she sneaks out, out from behind the walls that guard her. Lifting her head to the sun, she runs free, laughing with much gaiety. Letting her hair blow in the breeze and hugging the beauty of life, the lines of fear and hurt disappear for moments as the little girl she was emerges from within. The little girl who trusts and trusts. The little girl who looked at the world with her bright green eyes as a place of excitement and love and adventures. The little girl is so beautiful that when she is out, she can fill the world with her love and presence. But all too soon, she is gone, back into hiding. Hopefully she will emerge again, for the time in between is getting longer and longer. All I can do is wait for her to peek out once more.

Dianne, June 2001

I had started working for the church in 1989. We had moved from Illinois to Florida in the summer of 1984. We had three children at the time of the move, and I was pregnant with our fourth. A year later, we welcomed our fifth child. After the children were baptized, we attended mass weekly at our new parish. I felt guilty for not being able to put anything in the collection, so I decided to volunteer. I was introduced to one of God's greatest earthly angels, a beautiful nun. Sister Joyce ran the pastoral care ministry and the aging ministry. I still had three children at home, so my role was to drive seniors who could not drive to their meeting at church and home again. The kids and I loved doing this every week.

In 1987, we faced a crisis. Our son, who was nine at the time, was diagnosed with Tourette's syndrome. I had never heard of this neurological disorder, but I soon found out that not only did I not know about it, but neither did the school system. At that time, there were minimal resources available. This journey began. After educating myself, I would meet with teachers and explain the syndrome. When the teachers asked, I would give them workshops. A very special lady whom I met at church with would travel with me and give me the emotional support that was needed.

In 1989, my angel nun, Sister Joyce left the parish to work in another parish. My pastor at the time asked if I could fill in part time, covering the pastoral care ministry. It was February, and he needed me until Easter of that year. My prayers were answered because my son needed therapy, and I didn't know how I was going to pay for it. This position ended up lasting twelve years. In 1994, we received a new pastor, who asked me to work full time as the coordinator of pastoral care. My role was to travel with the priests to the hospitals, nursing homes, and the homebound, being the liaison between the parishioner and the priest. This was not my only responsibility; soon bereavement was added. It was decided that because of my visits and being a liaison, I could guide the families with their needs. I continued to learn and eventually became a facilitator who guided others on becoming ministers to the sick and bereavement ministers.

During this period in my life, I took the tools taught to me earlier in life and applied them to my ministry. I remembered my aunt wanting me to sit with her, not talking. I remembered a grandmother who wanted someone to listen to her and a grandfather who tried to drink himself to death because he didn't know how to fix his pain after the loss of his son and his wife.

Families have many trials, and I used to think it was God punishing us when the family had a trial. Soon I realized that when my children did something wrong, I wouldn't punish them or knock them down because they did something wrong. I wouldn't hurt them. I loved them and could never stop loving my children. That is how it is with God. God does not hurt us—God loves us.

We have choices, we have free will, and we must face the consequences of our actions and other individuals' actions. There is nothing more. However, God is there to give us the strength to face whatever life is dealing us. My role was to help others see God's love and strength in their lives. God has always been by my side, and He gives the strength to carry on. Even times when I could not pray, God was there. God was there in 1994 when my father passed away, and He was there in 1997 when I went through the divorce to save my life. God was there after the divorce. He gave me the strength in taking care of my children. In 1999, when my mother passed away, God gave me the strength to pray and hold her hand as she died.

God has provided the tools needed for my son. He is now an adult and is basically tic free.

God was with me when another son became very sick when he was five years old. After making many trips to the doctor's office and being sent home, they finally admitted him so they could get some sleep. His appendix ruptured in the middle of the night, and they rushed him into the operating room. He was in the hospital for eleven days. Today, he is married and has two children.

God was with me when my youngest daughter was four. She was diagnosed with tuberculosis of the lymph nodes. After many tests and treatment, she recovered. In grade school and high school, she was a basketball player and was ranked third in the state of Florida for three-point shooting. Then she blew out her knees. Life! She is married and has a daughter.

I have another son who is a sous-chef. As a child with many learning disabilities he overcame them by working hard. He ended up with a scholarship to a culinary school. He and his wife have two beautiful children.

My oldest daughter is always there for everyone, and she is the glue of the siblings. She keeps them together and updated. She and her husband have a daughter. She would help me with the younger children and was like their seconded mother. She is a strong woman, as were her namesakes. Her love for the world and people is infectious, but she does not even realize it.

I mention this because I am proud of my children. Their lives have not been easy, but they are passing their gifts on to their children— the gifts we received from our ancestors that are both biblical and heredity. They survived all the adversities in their lives, and they gave me life when I did not think I could go on. We worked together as a team after the divorce, and today we still work together. They value family, they value love, and they trust in God. They know without God, they would not have survived the adversities in their lives.

Life and Adversity

As life's problems soar, my faith enhances. Our whole beings, our whole lives begin, end, and begin again eternally with God. Our strengths are His because He is our heavenly Father. He instilled our values. Our faith is our loyalty. Pureness of faith begins inside. Outside forces try to destroy, but faith in the purest form is endless in its boundaries and provides all we need.

—Dianne, November 14, 1997

Chapter 6

DIGNITY

Over the years, I provided workshops throughout the country. The people I ministered to gave me insights into different aspects of Christ, from the laughing Christ to the broken Christ. My heart found a special place working with individuals involved with domestic violence. Below is a piece I wrote for a workshop I gave on domestic violence.

* * *

I would describe dignity as being able to look in the mirror and say, "No more!" To be able to see past the bruised heart and know that you are someone special, someone who deserves to be treated with love, with respect. Only you can let others take dignity from you. Only you can get it back again.

Dignity is knowing when you need to reach out to professionals for guidance. It is seeking out others and saying, "I need your help. I cannot do this alone."

Dignity is knowing that they are there to point you in the right directions, but not to do it for you. Only you can make this journey. Your priest, minister, rabbi, or counselor can only walk with you and encourage you.

When you start out on the journey to reclaim your dignity, steady your steps with faith and move forward. The journey is not easy and is filled with many twists and turns. It is filled with self-doubt and much humility. And, yes, the tears will flow like a river. But keep thinking of that person deep inside of you, the very being that was created in the image of God. The being that has been captive for so long and yearns to be free again as you move forward.

Then you take that first step of admittance, accepting the reality of what is happening to you. You begin to reclaim your dignity. As you reach out for guidance, a little more starts to seep in, and soon you don't want to stop because you want to reclaim more and more of the missing pieces of yourself.

Dignity is knowing that you broke the cycle of violence, and you have taught your children self-respect and how to respect others.

With dignity, you keep moving forward with your head held high through the good times and the bad, never running from life but embracing it. With dignity, you can walk away from any situation that demeans you because you know you are better than that. You don't do it with vengeance but instead walk away with pride. You stop enabling others to destroy the body of Christ within you. And one day you will be able to look at your children and let them see the risen Christ in you, not the broken Christ in you. You will show them dignity in Christ! Amen.

*   *   *

The women I worked with were stronger than they thought. I enjoyed watching them not only reclaim their lives but also advocate for others.

I became interested in this ministry when I realized there was a big misconception that people thought the church did not allow abused women to divorce. One of my goals was to educate the public that not only were there programs to help abused individuals, but one can divorce and have the marriage annulled if the body of Christ in you is being harmed. Many individuals were under the assumption they would be excommunicated from the church. Another misconception was that an annulment meant the marriage did not take place or the children were not legitimate. These are false statements.

Chapter 7

My Faith

My faith has always been who I am. It is figuring it out that is hard. I sit here on September 11, 2017, thinking. It was sixteen years ago today that our country realized we were vulnerable. Nothing like what happened on September 11, 2001, had ever happened before in our country. Two buildings destroyed by planes exploding, and thousands of people dying. I remember sitting in church and telling God how sorry I was for my greed that might have caused this. I'm used to air-conditioning and traveling by car. I am used to the freedom this country has to offer, and in one day it was threatened. I had to take a hard look at my life.

On the day of my first communion, our pastor stood at the pulpit and asked us to pray hard. It was October, and Cuba and the United States were on the brink of war. The fear of another war was always a threat in those days. It was fewer than twenty years since the ending of World War II. At school, we would have air raid drills and practice hiding under our seats. We would take field trips to the armory so we would know where to go if another war started or an atom bomb was dropped. I remembered how they stored commodities such as flour, water, sugar, and cheese. They were hidden in a place where we could go if there was a bombing. I remember being told to go to the building down by the river; it would be there we could find our parents. The food was to feed the town if we ended up there. When Father Gould asked us to pray that day (I was going to be seven in two weeks), all I could think of was, *I hope they have enough cheese for all of us.*

On the fateful day of September 11, 2001, I sat in church and told God I was sorry for how I took advantage of the life he gave me. I was sorry that I did not embrace my freedom and did not always find the good in others. You see, I did not want to pray on this day that I would have enough cheese. I knew the value now of my freedom and of my life.

Today, sixteen years later, I am sitting here and thanking God for the gift of life. Again, I am asking the direction to take it. Hurricane Irma came through last night. My town took a direct hit. When the wind and rain settled, my husband of eight years and I ventured out among the debris and trees that had fallen. One by one, our neighbors walked out, and we began the cleanup. I stood looking up and down the street as we worked side by side, People who I had argued with a few months ago, strangers I did not know, and elderly women were trying to help by doing whatever they physically could. We saw everyone pitching in, everyone smiling, and everyone thanking God we were all safe. Our lives had been threatened once more. With our world filled with hate and anger again, I had to stop and ask myself how much I contributed to the hate. Again, I am saying I'm sorry. Help me, God, to do better with the life You gave me.

How do you express yourself yet keep your cool? Life is human, and we are humans working toward enlightenment. It is not easy, but there are so many paths God provides for us. Believe it or not, the first one is each other. We have the means within each other. How do you see it, especially if you don't agree with each other? I talked about ego earlier. Our egos play such a part in our human lives. Who is prettier, who is richer, who is smarter, who is liked more, who is mistreated, who is bowed down to, who is in the lead, and who is behind? Who must follow, who is unsure, who must be right all the time, and who is responsible? Who doesn't care? Wow, I could continue forever. We label, we judge, we have expectations of others—and then we say we believe! I attended a mission years ago where a priest was talking about Lazarus. It was the start of my awakening. He talked about Jesus calling Lazarus out of the tomb, and then the priest asked two questions. "What tomb is Jesus calling you from? What is keeping you in the tomb?"

As we come across all individuals, we must listen to what Christ tells us. Some days, it is so hard because we have our way and our feelings, and we don't want to see our part or listen. I can remember one day, everything that could go wrong did, and it brought me to tears. My spiritual advisor called me and, in his spiritual advisor tone, said, "What is God telling you?"

Frustrated, I said, "Nothing, He knows I am so mad right now, I won't listen, so He is waiting for me to calm down." We all have days like that. We need to have a relationship with Christ. By that, I mean spend time with Him, pray (talk) with Him, and be comfortable in the silence with Him. It doesn't matter whether it's in times of sadness, anger, or fear, or even in times of rest. I will curl up in the womb of God and lie there, being comforted. I can rest, I can cry, I can be comforted, and then I can listen to the words of my creator, lover, and friend. Simply being embraced by the solace is restful to the soul. I must remind myself that as I can be embraced, so can everyone else who chooses.

One time I was having difficulty with someone at work. I went to mass, and there was the person. I thought, *Come on, God. How am I supposed to concentrate on You when they are here?*

God said, "Figure out how to live with each other, because you both are in the womb together." It hit me that it is not just me there—it's all of us, together. How do we get along? This is the famous question since day one. The evil one seems to enjoy trying to separate us from God. Did he not try to tempt Jesus? So we are not out of the woods. We must be on guard and defend the body of Christ not only in us but in each other. How do we do it?

We must look in the eyes of others, see the body of Christ, and open our eyes so they may see the body of Christ in us. You see, we are all made in the image of God. We have free will, so our behavior expresses that free will. Jesus showed us how to follow good and not evil. Jesus showed us how to live in love, and He gave us unconditional love. Evil will try to entice us away from God's love. We choose whom we want to follow.

> *As I stand held by evil, I hold my head high and with defiance boldly stare back into the eyes of evil. They hold me stripped naked, clothed only in humility. Their mockery will not touch me. I will prevail with all my strength. I will stand tall; I will hold my head high. I will not be defeated because I am strong with faith. They can take the very skin from my body, but they can never touch my soul.*

—Dianne, April 2001

Chapter 8

CHOICES

We have choices. Sometimes it means leaving, as hard as our choices can be. It is the Christ in us that needs to be taken care of. Sometimes the change means that you are not empowering others to destroy the body of Christ in you. You need to walk away. "What is keeping you in my tomb?" This question prompted me to get the help I needed and reclaim my dignity.

Over the next several years, as I grew in faith and confidence, I encountered problems I never dreamed of. I was dealing with being a single mom of five and the difficulties of running a house by myself. Every accomplishment was a gift, whether I was mowing the yard or fixing pipes. I was happy—the happiest I had ever been. I loved my job. I loved learning from the priests I worked with and from the spirituality they shared. I grew as a person and felt I was growing deeper in my spirituality. This also came from the people we ministered to. I knew that through God, I could make it.

It wasn't long after the divorce that the age-old problems of jealousy, fear, power, and hate—the very same vices that crucified Jesus—started to spin, and I found myself the center of gossip. All good things can be marred by gossip. People perceive what they want to perceive, and people like to believe the perceptions. Rumors started flying. The major one was I'd divorced my husband to be with a priest. No matter what I said, people want to believe what they want to believe, regardless of whether it is true.

A couple of years later, I found myself starting to panic, and I was afraid. I was afraid of losing something else in my life, as well as my ministry. During this time, my mother passed away. Suddenly I felt as though my world was crumbling. I couldn't understand why people could be so mean. I felt like I was drowning in loss. I went to my mentor and facilitator and said, "I didn't know what to do." I was in my second year of pastoral ministries with one more year to go. I didn't think I could continue.

She informed me that the only way to put an end to the gossip about me and the hatred would be if they transferred the priest, if the person gossiping left, or if I left my position. Well, I knew the answer: it was time for me to leave the safety of my job. She reassured me I could finish out the following year and become commissioned as a pastoral minister. I didn't want to mention this to anyone until I made my decision. I prayed hard, and I cried hard. Soon I was offered a position developing support groups for individuals who were blind or losing their sight due to macular degeneration. After much prayer, I accepted the position and turned in my resignation. My third child had just graduated from high school, and I had two more to go. I was scared, and my support group was gone. It was me and God, and boy, did I lean on God. I knew I had no one to turn to now. This was it.

The Jump!

Faith in God is plunging into the unknown while knowing God has a plan for you. It's being afraid that it's hurting so bad, you can't breathe. It's jumping off a cliff but knowing God will catch you. It's saying, I don't want to do this, but I will because I trust You, God. And I know this is what You want of me. I don't know why You want this or the purpose, but I will answer Your call. I will answer Your call. I know You will comfort my tears, and Your purpose will unfold. I'm ready—let's go. Hold me, love me. I am Yours. I love You and trust You. I'm jumping now, God.

—Dianne, August 2001

The Catch!

I have taken the plunge, and You, my Father, have caught me. You set me down gently into Your world of beauty. As I journey with You, I see a world of great wonderment, a world so beautiful and filled with Your wonder. You have taken me into a world where light can only be seen inside the soul. You have shown me how to see without eyes. You have taken me into the souls of others, where they have shown me You. I now understand that I have been the one blind, but my eyes are open now. I came into a world where there are so many holy men and women. These men and women not trying to be holy or preaching the words of the Gospel but are living the Gospel and just being. By doing so, they're fulfilling Your expectations and preaching the Gospel through their actions. Thank You, God, for taking care of me.

—Dianne, August 2001

Chapter 9

A New Journey with God

In August 2001, I started a new journey. What beautiful journey it was. I got to see the world differently. I got to see the world through the blind. I didn't start just the three support groups as they asked. I started eight groups across three counties. These groups were run by the people supporting each other. From these groups came education to the community. We would go and speak. We would teach, and we would give each other a purpose. There was one individual, and I didn't know whether he wanted to take a class. I asked him, "Besides driving a car, what else do you want to do?"

He said, "Go to a shooting range."

I said, "Okay, let's go." I got permission, and we went.

After that, he said, "I just had to try shooting once more," That was the last time he went to the shooting range. He made up his mind to live, and live he did. He attended training on the cane, how to use computers, and how to live on his own. He ended up working in the store at the school, and there he met the love of his life. They were married a short time later. I love watching God's miracles.

This position ended in 2003, and once more I was thrown into the unknown. My fourth child graduated from high school and was in culinary school when I was offered a position in pastoral care at a parish about an hour away. God's plan for me continued. At first, I planned on commuting, but after a few months, I put the house on the market, and away we went. New job, new community, new life.

Strength

What is our strength? We only understand mortal strength. The strength from God is beyond all comprehension because we must have proof. How many times have we said, "How did I do that? I never thought I could get through this." Our strengths stretch beyond our imagination. We move our mountains with faith. Faith in God's love is all we need. It's there even if we don't ask because our heavenly Father wills it.

—Dianne, January 1997

Chapter 10

MOVING ON WITH GOD

Police Chaplain

After taking the job in pastoral care at the new parish and moving to a new town, I found I had several new journeys waiting for me. My role was to oversee the ministry to the sick and the bereavement ministry. Again, I felt the need to give back and this time to my community. I enrolled in a program that certified me to be part of a domestic abuse response team. I was asked a short time later to join the chaplains board as a civilian. They felt my expertise in pastoral care would be a great benefit. Several months later, the head chaplain asked me to be a chaplain. I explained to him I was not ordained. He said he wanted someone who could be available to give death notification. I explained I had to get permission from my diocese. The head of pastoral care gave me the permission and a letter that explained why I was qualified, so my training began.

My training involved several classes on death and death notification. I also learned proper safety techniques. I traveled all over the United States for these classes. I met chaplains from all over the world. One of the things we were required to do was a ride-along.

This required riding with officers for their shifts. This experience was unbelievable. Not only did it offer the law enforcement an opportunity to vent, but it showed me what they face every day. I think of all the times I did a ride-along, the scariest was when I was in another state. When I first got in the police car, the officer asked if I'd ever shot a shotgun. I told him, "Yes, a few times in Illinois target practicing." He unlocked his shotgun and said, "If something happens, use it." All I could think was, *Um, this is not good.* Luckily, I never needed it, but it was rough out there. I saw many drug busts and domestic violence calls. I was a volunteer in this ministry for ten years. Unfortunately, the last few years were hard due to health reasons and ongoing back surgeries.

One thing I learned from being a police chaplain was that all faiths and all beliefs have the same major themes: love, and the fact that evil will try to invade. One time I was called to the hospital to be with a mother whose six-year-old son was run over. When I got there, I was taken to a room with a mother and a translator. The mother was from another country and was of another faith. I explained why I was there and asked her if she could teach me a prayer because I was Catholic and did not know any prayers in her faith. I explained I too was a mother and was here to support and pray with her. She taught me a prayer through the translator, and we prayed the prayer. She then asked me to teach her one of my prayers, so I taught her the "Our Father." A few minutes later, the doctor came in and said, "I can't explain this, but we can't find any injuries." There were no injuries. Praise God, the beauty of prayer. There were numerous stories, but that one always stuck with me.

I ministered to people of all faiths, color, status, and race. People were in shock and hurting, but in the middle of tragedy, everyone would come together. I admit I shed many tears and spent a lot of time on the ground rocking people. One night I was consoling a grandmother whose grandson was involved in a gang shooting. She said she had something to do, and I followed her outside and across the street to where a large group of people had gathered. It was the friends of her grandson. She begged them to stop and not retaliate. She was tired of the killing. I witnessed a grandmother in the middle of the night begging for peace. They listened to her pleas and did not retaliate out of respect for her.

Children were always the hardest. It is so hard to understand, but where I found solace was the understanding that children fulfilled the Gospel message by being. That is all God asks of us: to be and to love. The amount of love that a child brings is amazing. God weeps with us. It is strange that the death of a child is what took me from God, but it was through that death that Jesus came to bring me back to Him. Ever since then, it was the children's families I attended to, and it was the children I prayed over and for. It was the children I cried for as I rocked their lifeless bodies. I have made the sign of the cross with their parents' tears as they said goodbye. I remember these children on the Feast of Holy Innocents when, during a special prayer service, we place an ornament on a Christmas tree for all the little ones in heaven.

When you work in these ministries—whether it is at the hospital with the sick and the dying, or the couple who suffered the death of their baby, or with a young wife who's just lost her husband—you have to take care of yourself. You cannot be everything to everyone, and this is not your work; it is God working through you. People would ask me, "How do you do this day after day?"

My response was, "I don't—God does. I am just an instrument that said, 'Yes, God.'"

Another journey I was not expecting was marriage. Ten years after my divorce, I remarried. I began a new journey of blending two lives. It was not easy at first because I had become independent. My children were grown. Even though I'd said, "Never again," I said, "I do." We both pray every day for guidance because marriage takes three: me and my husband, and the center is God. Without God, we could not make it.

The Gifts of God

The gifts of God to us are different to those we touch; that is what makes us unique. Our gifts can affect one person one way and another person in a different way, even though it's the same gift. Those who enter our lives have a special purpose, whether they are positive or negative. We need to be open to the gifts of others and share our gifts with others.

—Dianne, March 1998

Chapter 11

MY INVENTORY

Over the years, I continued to minister at various parishes in Lakeland. The joy of being able to guide others in the ministry is a gift. There are ups and downs in working in a parish, but the ups outweigh the downs any time. We are called to journey with our parishioners and guide them. We do not dictate or criticize. We show love, and we show God's love for them. We are all sinners traveling this journey. We make mistakes. We ask for forgiveness as well as forgive. We know when to walk away when things cannot be changed. We are called to pray for those who hurt us. We try not to get caught up in the dramas of life, but we do. We try not to get angry or hurt or mad, but we do. We try not to hurt, but we do. We stop and say, "I am sorry, I was wrong. I am sorry I hurt you or got angry."

But we don't stop there. We must ask ourselves, "Why did I get angry? Was I afraid? Was I threatened? Did I react to my past? What is my part in this? Was I sick or in pain? Did I overwork and not take enough breaks?" No, I am not making excuses. I am examining myself to see why I reacted that way. Now I must figure out what I need to do to better take care of myself. You see, I cannot change another person. I cannot change the way others act. I can only change the way I react to the situation. Again, this is not easy.

My ego gets in the way all the time. This is a struggle I work on. It is hard to look at yourself and see your own faults, but I have found that most of the time, it brings me peace. The other times, I must be honest with myself until I can find that peace. Usually it is because I don't like myself at that time, or I keep looking back. This is usually the problem. Once I realize what I am doing and why, I work to fix myself, and then I find peace. Before we can love others, we need to love ourselves. Before we can forgive others, we need to forgive ourselves. In doing so, we come closer into the realm of God. We come into a peaceful, loving relationship with ourselves and a deeper relationship with God. Our relationship with God will always go much deeper than we can possibly believe.

God Rejoices in Us

God is present not only in times of trouble but also in our joys and victories. We tend to forget this because in the good times, we feel like we are in control. We seek out God. In bad times, we know we aren't in control. We seek out God. God wants to celebrate the good times. Close your eyes and feel God's hug for you.

—Dianne, April 1998

Chapter 12

IT IS TIME FOR LISTENING

Today I have been reflecting over the years. I have been married to my husband for eleven years. My children are grown. I have had numerous procedures and back surgeries that make it so difficult to walk some days. Back in 1997, I dealt with the stress of my divorce and the deaths of my father. The neurologists diagnosed me with fibromyalgia in 1997, which causes severe muscle pain.

I had to retire in the summer of 2018 to prepare for another fusion. My husband has been a wonderful caregiver and a great support through all this. My mother, bless her soul, always said, "Offer your pain for those souls in purgatory." Well, I can unofficially tell you that purgatory is clear. Just joking, Bishop! In the Catholic faith, purgatory is a place where, after death, we go to purify ourselves before we meet God. We also do this through the sacrament of reconciliation. We need to constantly look at ourselves and see where we need to purify ourselves. We need to look at our action, words, and thoughts. Do we see Christ in others? Do we walk away from conflict that is hurtful not only to us but to others? Do we hurt others with our words? Do we treat everyone as equal? Do we pray? We need to pray. We need to pray for ourselves. We need to pray for others, especially those who hurt us. We need to pray for our world!

Retirement is not easy for me. I get so frustrated over what I can't do. I want to go for walks with my grandchildren. I want to travel and see things. But I must remind myself that my ministry now is listening. I volunteer at church, running grief support groups. I try to teach others what I have learned so that the lessons can be carried on. I was feeling bad one day when my older grandchildren were visiting. I was trying to think of things we could do until my grandson said, "Grandma, we like coming and sitting on the porch with you. We can talk about things, and we talk about feelings and stuff." Wow, whoever thought they didn't want to be entertained? They wanted to talk and be heard.

Sometimes the things that frustrate us the most are God saying, "Sit and listen to the world around you." This recalls the Bible story of Martha and Mary. There is a time to work and a time to listen. My life is not over; it is simply changing again. It is time to listen. It is time to listen to the birds and chipmunks. It is time to watch the sun rise and the sun set. It is a time to listen to others. It is time to reflect and write. It is time to sit and listen to God!

Christ's Light

I sit and listen to the peaceful sounds of the night. When I look up, I see the stars sparkling in the darkness. They remind me of the light of Christ. As I enter the night of my life, I see the sparkle of Christ's light like the stars, lighting a path of love, hope, and comfort. It is in that sparkle that I feel the embrace and the glow penetrate deep within my soul and radiate out from me with love.

—Dianne, April 2002

Some Miscellaneous Thoughts and Prayers from My Journal

Tranquility

Diamonds sharp enough to cut glass. Sharp enough to cut through evil bindings. Stars reflect blue diamonds in the distance. Diamonds that are coming to cut the binds of evil. Soon I will be free. I see light from afar, and I know my Father has sent the sword surrounded by the light to free me. The night reflects the light of the blue diamond's coming with my Father's love given through the blue diamond's light, and I will be freed by his sword.

And then one by one, the bindings around the heart of the green emeralds are released. The courageous words from the blue diamond knight sliced through the treasure of the green emeralds. Once the last binding was cut, the soul was now free.

The knight, with so much courage, cut through the bindings releasing her soul, her treasure. And she was free. She will always hold in her heart the blue diamond knight, for he was sent to her by God, and the green emeralds shine again with life and confidence.

—Dianne, May 2001

His Eyes

Almighty God,

I sit here in wonder. The wonder of the beauty You have given us. In the sky, the trees, the water, the flowers, and all the animals. I wonder with so much beauty, how do we miss the eyes of You?

The eyes of the poor, the eyes of the mistreated, the eyes of the fearful, the eyes of the hungry, the eyes of the injustice, the eyes wanting to be heard, the eyes wanting to give live, the eyes of the bullied, the eyes seeking forgiveness, the eyes needing love, the eyes wanting to give love, the lowered eyes of shame, and the raised eyes in prayer. Eyes searching for answers, eyes of hope, eyes of faith, eyes of love.

Open my eyes, Lord, so I may see Your eyes in others. Open my eyes so they can see You in me … and then teach us to walk hand in hand into Your eyes, which is oneness with You!

We ask this through Your Son, Jesus the Christ. Amen.

—Dianne, 2017

The Beginning of My Bereavement Ministry

The beginning of my bereavement ministry was a great conversion. A close friend of mine lost her grandchild. I was so angry that God could take such a little one. I would not even buy a card that mentioned God or God's love. I went with friends to the funeral but was still angry. I sat not listening to the priest. When they carried the little casket down, the tears flowed down my face.

During the homily, I suddenly became very warm—not earthy heat but a peaceful warmth. And then there was a light. It was as though time had stopped. In the light and warmth, Jesus suddenly appeared. He picked up the baby, who was laughing, and cuddled him. He looked at me and said, "I will take care of him." He then went to the parents and grandparents and told them the same thing, but they did not seem to hear him. He looked at me again and smiled, and then He was gone. Suddenly the light was gone, and I became cold.

I looked around to say, "Did you see that?" but no one was acting any different; they were listening to the homily. The homily was ending, and I felt peaceful and very much in touch with God. It was so beautiful that I cannot properly describe it. This happened around 1991, but it is so impressed in my mind. It was the most beautiful experience I have ever had. I promised God I would continue my bereavement ministry and would try to help others see His beauty. To this day, I see the saints and feel their presence when I am at a death. It is so beautiful to see the spirits rise to great each other. To feel their holy appearance is beyond description. It engulfs me in beauty and peace. I simply smile and say goodbye!

—Dianne, November 2001

The Crucifix

I was confused and needed guidance from my Father, so I locked myself in my room and prayerfully called to my Abba for help. I entered the embrace. I transcended from my mortal body into the energy of God. While there, I came to a cross, and on the cross was a man—my brother Jesus. I was looking over His shoulder; it was more gruesome than I could imagine. He was bleeding, and the smell of sweat and blood was strong. His head hung forward, His eyes were defeated, and His chest was sunken in. The sight of Him tore at my being. Tears rolled down my face. All I kept hearing was, "If you are going to follow Me, you are going to die many times." I knew that to truly follow my brother I must die the deaths on the cross. I told Him I loved Him, and I cried. I was there with Him. The look, the odor, cannot be explained. His death was barbaric. The road to belief is many deaths in Jesus's name and example. I so love Him, as He loves me. I was in communion with Jesus as He hung on the cross—not in fantasy but in reality.

—Dianne, February 2001

The Weed

I needed answers. I was lost. After a meeting, I decided to walk the track, but I made it as far as the bleachers. I looked toward the heavens and called out to God. "Tell me, please, what You want from me." I looked down, and there was a weed sticking straight up, taller than the grass. It was straight and strong, but it was out of place. Upon looking closer at the grass where the weed was rooted, I noticed how the grass intertwined to form a blanket of beauty. A beauty God created. I had to ask myself, Am I the weed standing alone, or the grass intertwined with others? Or maybe I'm like the weed: by standing taller, it brought me to look closer at God's beauty. I need to be the weed by being willing to rise high and draw others to look closer to the beauty of God that surrounds us.

—Dianne, September 2000

Past, Present, Future

The silence is broken by a gentle breeze. The trees sway, bringing together the musical sound of nature. Birds call to each other in a language all their own.

The ripples on the water hypnotize your senses.

Gazing out across the water, to the boundaries surrounding the past, present and the future lay spread before the human eye.

The dead trees remind me of the past. They served their purpose; now it is time to make way for the future. Slowly they fall. A branch here and a branch there. No growth, just a reminder.

The strong, sturdy trees stand tall, providing shade and respite. The present serving a purpose.

The new little trees sprouting with eager anticipation, the future.

All important to nature, for the old provided the stability till the young could stand tall. The tall and sturdy provides the new growth so the cycle can continue.

All the beauty of God stretching before our eyes. Nothing can destroy it except man.

Will greed take the past, present, and future?

—Dianne, March 6, 2003

Intimacy

How do I begin to describe my intimacy with God? I have just returned from a three-week spiritual vacation. This is a jubilee year, and I returned to my home, my roots. There, I found the gift of me. I forced myself to remember my life. I forgave those who hurt me, laughed with those who loved me, and embraced the roots of my life. I also found that through my life, I embraced justice. Whether befriending individuals of color in our small town as true friends (not as a novelty), challenging the school board for women's sports in school (which was implemented the year after my graduation), or petitioning the city council at the age of sixteen for a parade to honor our Vietnam vets (which they granted, and we had a successful homecoming), the questions for me were not "Why?" but "Why not?" Whether black, white, female, or male, we are all equal—equal not among ourselves but equal to God, for we are all made in God's image.

—Dianne, June 2000

Discipleship

To understand our discipleship is to spread the message and love of God. We must face the challenges of life. To hide or surround ourselves with the comfortable is to deny our God among us. For God is not only in us but in others. The very being of our lives is God's presence. To shield from the pain and fears is to shield ourselves from God.

—Dianne, August 2000

The Womb of God

I am engulfed in the womb of God. Here, I am sustained. At times I feel separated from the human body, as though I am peering from the outside to see where my spirituality is to go and be perceived. How do I explain? This is beyond words! God is my very being, which I am sustained. To feel God is unexplainable. Feeling God's love and embrace is beyond human comprehension. It is a total surrendering that engulfs my very being. It is being lifted beyond the bounds of mortality into divine love. It is a pleasure of ecstasy of incomprehension. Being totally engulfed with the divine love is a joy of joys. I long to stay in the embrace but know I must return to bring others. For the kingdom to be complete is to unite all in a oneness of the ecstasy of God's love. Divine love cannot be described except for complete. We are all called to join in divine love.

—Dianne, September 2000

Beautiful Day with God

Today was a beautiful day, a spiritual, loving day. We had two hospital visits. One lady had a stroke, but during the prayers, the love of the Spirit poured forth. The second visit was a young woman going for a mastectomy; her husband joined in the prayers and wept as we prayed. We also had two funerals. During these times, everything we've prepared for, from baptism on, comes forth. How these times are handled is our faith. All the homilies and all the study bring forth our belief now and being there is so spiritual. I never want to lose these moments. I hope to be able to continue to be part of God's love for others. I feel so lucky God chose me to do this ministry.

—Dianne, 1997

Bishop's Anointing

I will be commissioned as a certified pastoral minister. With oil, our bishop will anoint my hands to do great things for God. My Father calls me into a realm others do not understand because they do not see as I do. I must bring them into the light. Even though they reject me, they will know they are being touched by the hands of God, for I am not an individual but an extension of God. I will radiate the ministry and love of our Father because I am not alone on this journey. God is my guide.

—Dianne, May 2002

Butterfly

Recently, a very dear friend of mine expressed on her death bed that she hoped she could come back as a butterfly. I could not help but think what a beautiful analogy of death and life.

The inside of a cocoon is safe. It provides a protective covering over the moth that lives inside. Like our bodies. Through a process of transformation, a beautiful butterfly emerges into a life unknown. Through the transformation, the beauty of the butterfly is brought to its full magnificence—just as in our death and resurrection, we are brought to our full magnificence!

Thank you, Dear Barb for the gift of your friendship. You will always be in my heart dear friend.

—Dianne, April 2018

Wings

The wings of angels shield us from the blows. When we falter in faith, we feel pain. Our faith wards off the sting of the blows encountered in living life.

—Dianne, 1998

Emotions

Words cannot describe the emotions I am feeling today. No one will ever be able to understand. Eight years ago, I knew I had to take a stand. I was afraid but knew that in order to claim my soul and my life, I had to leave my marriage. My children were ten, twelve, fourteen, seventeen, and nineteen. I did not know how I was going to make a life for us, but I knew I would. These past eight years have been a struggle and full of adversity. My goal was to get them out of high school in one piece and not be destroyed by all the problems. Today, I accomplish the goal. Karlie, my youngest, graduates today—with honors. Two graduated with scholarships. And two graduated with GPA honors. I did it, and tomorrow begins a new journey. God has been my companion, my friend, and my guide. Others have been my stability and encouragement; they were the human touch of God's love to see me through.

—Dianne, May 18, 2005

Hell

Sometimes the holy is not so grand and beautiful. I am being toyed with by evil. I have been plummeted into hell. As I crawl to reach the surface again, the evil one mocks me from the side and shoves me back again. He tries to steal my soul from God. He can't and won't, because my faith rests in my Father's womb. As I claw to the top, tear-stained and dirty, he sits with a smirk and asks if I have had enough yet.

Bleeding and bruised, I will keep climbing. He mocks me when friends come to help; he blocks their entrance. With defiance in my eyes, I glare at him and keep moving forward. As I feel human life being drained from me, the soul gets stronger. As I grow weary and am wracked with pain, I will continue to move toward God. When I am discouraged or afraid, I curl up into the safety of Abba's womb. Evil cannot and will not prevail. Lord, walk with me, shield me, and give me strength. When others see a dead body, let them see the live soul in Your divine embrace.

—Dianne, April 30, 2001

The Sacred Heart

The sacred heart of Jesus is the world. It is all of us encased within the heart. We are one with God. The thorns around the heart are our constant rejection of our oneness with God. The thorns will disappear when love encases us all and we move in love and oneness to the unity of the divine love … God.

Jesus carries us all in his heart, not separately but as one. We need to pull the thorns from the heart with unity of our love in oneness.

Though we are separate, we are one!

—Dianne, 2000

The Road to the Tabernacle

This is an individual prayer that I wrote for Holy Thursday. The road to the tabernacle was a path consisting of rocks placed by parishioners in front of the Tabernacle, which was in a place of private prayer. Before the parishioner sat down, he or she placed a rock, saying this prayer.

Dear God,

As I sit here today, mixed emotions wash over me. I listen to the readings and hear the message to forgive, but it is hard. I have suffered humiliation and hurt.

I want to move forward and forgive, but my heart feels wrapped in stone and that keeps me from you. I yearn for the freedom of this heaviness. I want to begin the steps toward forgiveness.

As we prepare as a community to bring our gifts before you let me bring a gift, this stone, as a symbol of the stone around my heart.

My stone can begin to form a road. A road that will provide the freedom of the past, a road that will put me in the present and a road that will lead me into the future

As I start to lay the road, I remember that you forgave the others that hurt and betrayed you. Give me the strength to remove this stone and guide me with your light as I journey down this new road of forgiveness.

Lord, I do not seek vengeance on the one or ones who have caused me hurt. Your healing is available to all. I pray that you shed your light to guide me to forgiveness, healing and peace of heart. Amen

—Dianne, Holy Thursday Night, 2016

Holy Innocents

I wrote the following reflection for the Feast of Holy Innocence. This feast day is December 28. On this day, we remember all the children killed by Herod. Herod ordered all the children ages two and under killed in the hopes of killing Jesus. On this day, we also remember all children who have died throughout the world.

A specific prayer service I developed when I worked at one of the parishes involved placing an undecorated Christmas tree in the grotto. Since then, whatever church I am ministering at, I either place the tree in the sanctuary or outside. This tree is not decorated with the rest of the Christmas trees. It stays bare until December 28, which is the Feast Day of the Holy Innocents. Then on the evening of December 28, we have a prayer services, and after hearing the readings of the day, I will usually give a reflection. At the end of the reflection, I invite parents who have lost a child to place an ornament on the bare tree. It does not matter the age or how long ago the death was. This includes children who have died from an accident, illness, still birth, miscarriage, abortion, or natural causes. This allows the parents or other family members to celebrate and honor their children. After all ornaments are placed on the tree, the tree is lit, and the beauty of all the little angels shine! This does not replace the Feast of Holy Innocents but adds to it. Below is the first reflection I wrote; it was given at the first prayer service we did with the angel Christmas tree. This took place in the year 1999.

Reflection for Holy Innocents

Some of the most heart-wrenching calls we receive are the ones that involves a child that has died, or a family has suffered a miscarriage. Even though these are difficult calls, they are the most sacred and holy. When I hold that lifeless child in my arms or look into the eyes of the parents who had a miscarriage, I see sacredness. I see a path of holiness and faith we are all called to walk. All God asks of us is to love one another, to come together as one in communion with Jesus the Christ for the kingdom of God. I look with awe as I realize this tiny child has been able to fulfill this. When I look around the room, I see family, friends, priest, nurses, and our faith community coming together in prayer and offering love, support, and comfort. Everyone comes together as one as they also call out to our Lord for strength and comfort. All personal agendas are suspended for a time. It's a time to bring the human touch of God's love to the family. How is this so different from any other death? These beautiful children were able to evangelize the word of God by bringing love and giving love. They do this by just <u>being.</u> These little ones, whether a few weeks in womb or several months, no matter the age, were able to accomplish in a short time what some have never been able to do. They were able to proclaim the gospel message and bring others together as one, for the kingdom of God. These children did this by simply being. They were tiny lights that sparked that great flame of love in others.

On this feast day, we are reminded of the children who died so the Word of God would live. Innocent babies slaughtered because a king felt threatened. A king afraid he would lose power, be overshadowed, or be inconvenienced. Babies who died from a senseless and selfish act. I find it overwhelming that some two thousand years later, on this day we remember all babies who are still dying from senseless and selfish acts. With that tiny light that glows also from these very little ones, they are bringing an awareness to the value of life and calling others to respond to the value of life.

As I stand here tonight and look upward to the stars, I think of all the little ones whose lights of love have touched me. These tiny lights of love remind me of another light that announced the word of God. "A star." A star in Bethlehem that shone brightly above a dirty, dark, cold stable where two parents were plunged into uncertainty and fear. But they had faith and trusted in God. I think of a star that shined above a manger that held a beautiful little boy, who loved us so much He would die someday so we could have everlasting life.

As difficult as these calls are, I wouldn't trade them for anything because these little ones, whose lights shine as bright as the Christmas star, remind me that the light of Christ shines in all of us. I hope I can live up to the example of faith and love these little ones have shown me.

—Dianne, 1999

What Is Love?

Love goes much deeper than idle words.
Love joins two souls, and the souls unite with God as one,
And all are united with the kingdom.

Love between a man and a woman is a special
love that runs deep beyond the outer layer of
human existence.

It is submerging one being with another being
And emerging the two beings as one.
Though they will always be individuals,
their very beings are immersed with the other being.

It is a beautiful feeling; it is God shining through the other.
To truly love someone this deep is to love God to the fullest,
For it is Christ who is the center of the being.
—Dianne, 2000

Now I will close with an invitation to you my readers:

Come give me your hand and let me gaze into your eyes so I may see Christ and look into my eyes and see Christ … and then let us walk hand in hand into the oneness with God!

Thank you, and may God bless you.
—Dianne, 2019

CPSIA information can be obtained
at www.ICGtesting.com
Printed in the USA
BVHW031800101119
563400BV00002B/8/P